ART WITH HEART PRESENTS

CHILL + SPILL

A PLACE TO PUT IT DOWN AND WORK IT OUT

Written by Steffanie Lorig and Jeanean Jacobs, MA, ATR-BC, LPAT, CPC

Designed by Andrew Wicklund

With Special Thanks to:
Ron Rabin, MA, LMHC, Jane V. Tillman, LMHC, and Rosalie Frankel, MA, ATR
for their invaluable contributions and for vetting this book.

This book is dedicated to all the teens and 'tweens
who just need a quiet place to
scream, dream, doodle, noodle,
evaluate, deliberate, realize + visualize.

An **evaluation study** report on the benefits of Chill & Spill
is available by contacting us at info@artwithheart.org.

Proceeds from the sale of this book, as well as your generous **donations**,
help support the mission of Art with Heart. Please send your contribution to:
Art with Heart, P.O. Box 94402, Seattle, WA 98124-6702,
or donate online at www.artwithheart.org/donate.

ART WITH HEART is focused on helping youth who are adversely affected by hardship and stress, healing emotional wounds through evidence-based therapeutic and interactive books and curriculum.

We are unique in the nonprofit world, acting as a catalyst for world-class collaborations between mental health experts and award-winning artists to create life-changing tools that benefit youth, increasing their emotional health and well-being so they can thrive despite hardships. Your support makes our outreach possible: **artwithheart.org**.

Chill & Spill was developed by Art with Heart in collaboration with therapists and psychologists.

ISBN 978-0-9841365-5-1. Chill & Spill: A Place to Put It Down & Work It Out. Published by Art with Heart Press. ©2013 Art with Heart. All rights reserved. First Printing: August 2005. Second Printing: February 2010. Third Printing: January 2011. **Fourth Printing: May 2013.** Cover Illustration by Mark Todd. Design by Andrew Wicklund.

Artwork by David Lemley

3

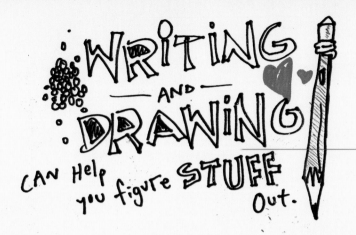

WRITING — AND — DRAWING CAN Help you figure STUFF Out.

It really can. Just try it! This journal is **your** place to chill out and spill your guts. It's a place to explore how you honestly feel, not just today, but everyday.

You aren't doing this to please anyone else...no one is judging you on how well you draw or write. It's an outlet for all the stuff you've got bottled up inside. Use this book to talk out **LOUD**, to say things you gotta say – it's your safe place to yell, cry, boast, dream and evolve.

As you go through Chill & Spill, notice what mood you're in. Change colors as your mood changes. Once this book is filled up, keep doodling on every bit of scrap paper you can find... 'cause the more you express yourself, the clearer things get. And the clearer things get, the stronger you'll be.

Start on the next page. Write down whatever's on your mind. Write about what happened today – even about what you had for lunch if you want to. Or just doodle away! Be sure to write the date next to each entry so you can look back and see how far you've come.

NO RULES. EVERYTHING'S COOL!!!

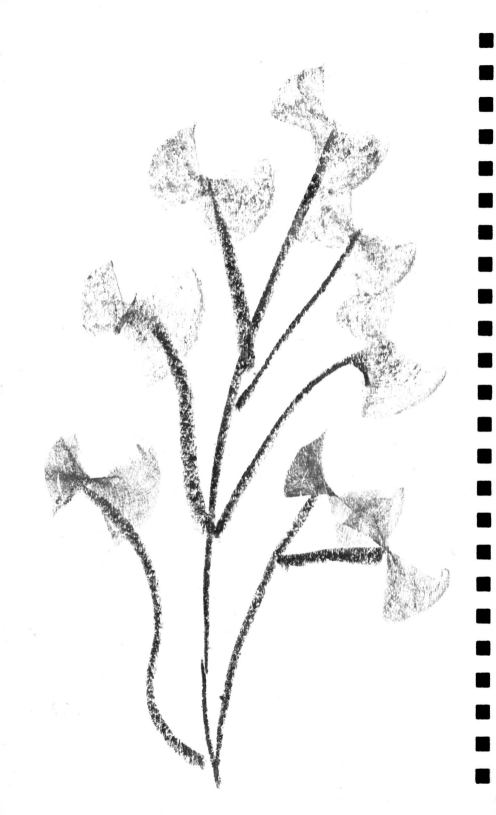

Artwork by Mary Jones

FLYaway

Imagine you are a small seed that has been picked up by a bird who takes you far, far away and places you somewhere safe. Imagine that you take root and start growing. How big do you get? What kind of plant do you become? What other kinds of plants are nearby? Who discovers and tends to you? Draw where you are and what you look like.

REMEMBER: This is not an art contest... you can draw cartoons, stick figures, ballpoint doodles, whatever. It's all cool.

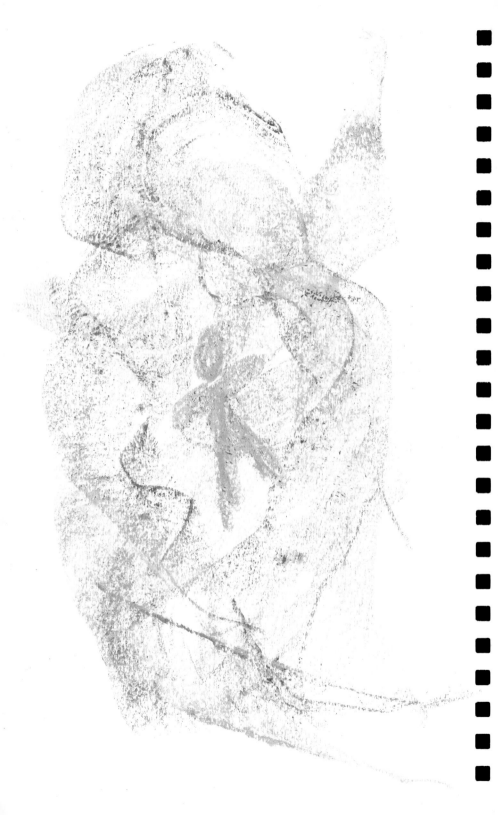

9

You are a reporter for a celebrity magazine. Interview yourself and write an article about who you are. Make sure to ask some of these important questions:

Exclusive Interview

What are your talents and strengths?

What really bothers you?

What advice would you give someone else in the same situation?

What is the most important thing in your life right now?

What things are you most proud of?

Where do you want to be in 5 years and what will you be doing?

If you could change the world in one way, what would you do and why?

Think of other questions too and include them in your story. Draw a picture that captures the spirit of this Exclusive Interview!

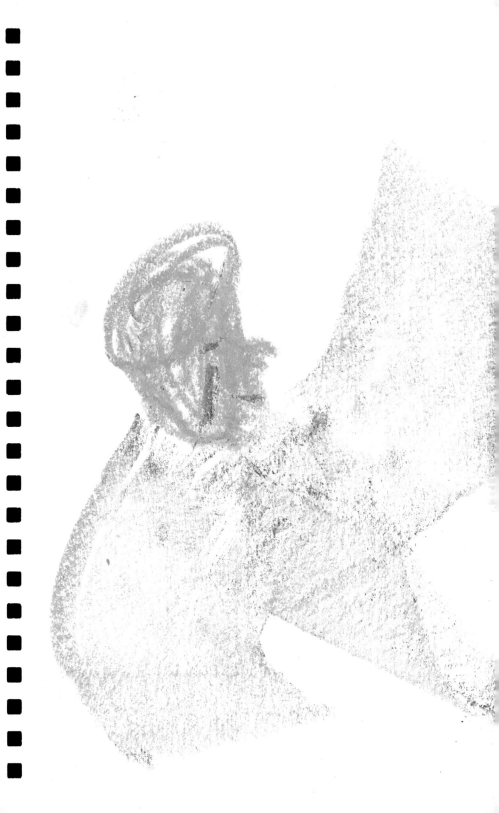

Artwork by Katherine Streeter

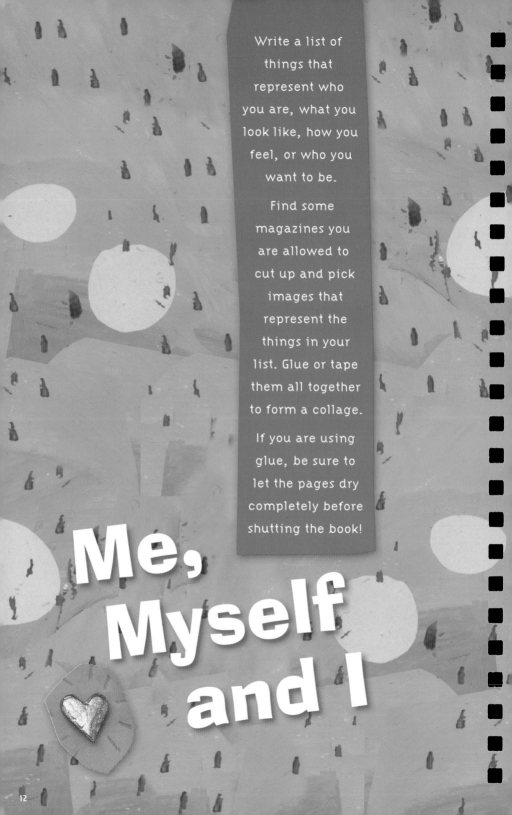

Write a list of things that represent who you are, what you look like, how you feel, or who you want to be.

Find some magazines you are allowed to cut up and pick images that represent the things in your list. Glue or tape them all together to form a collage.

If you are using glue, be sure to let the pages dry completely before shutting the book!

Me, Myself and I

and I really, really do FEEL that way.

I decided to say and say and say

always Never ever

Especially Using the prompts below, start writing on the next page, letting your imagination flow freely. Don't think too hard about it or censor yourself. Write several sentences for each one.

I want... I need... I fear... I wish...
I hope... I expect... I am... I love...

Review what you wrote, circling things that stick out to you. Draw a picture or write a poem using those words as a starting point.

I hope all I said was and sho

Artwork by Lilla Rogers

and pain

I so wish because

You

the hardest part

didn't you know that about ME?

Rogers

14

Fill in this mandala with colors that represent your feelings about the change of seasons.

Artwork by Dushan Milic

On
the next page,
make your own mandala by
drawing a target with three circles
(see above). In the middle circle, draw
things that represent your strengths. In
the next ring, draw what you are fearful of.
Next, fill the outer ring with positive ways
you can deal with your fears. Keep making
other mandalas by dividing circles into
equal shapes and picking other themes
to explore (balance, love, strength,
safety, community, peace,
change, etc.).

CIRCLE JOURNEY CIRCLE JOURNEY CIRCLE JOURNEY CIRCLE JOURNEY

Artwork by Nate Williams

17

iNsIde oF me

MAP OF MY HEAD: Lots of things go through your head all the time. Make a map showing things that are on your mind today. Come back to this section every day this week and map out different things you are thinking about each day.

MAP OF MY HEART: Draw a heart and inside it, write (or draw) the different emotions you feel today. Include as many as you can think of. Here's a list of words to help you get started: joyful, trusting, afraid, surprised, anxious, optimistic, disappointed, creative, blocked, proud, ashamed, smart, confused, hopeful, excited, frustrated, nervous, goofy, serious, peaceful, irritated. **What are some other words that describe your heart today?**

Artwork by Mark T. Smith

Artwork by Steffanie Lorig

POWER full

POW er less

Using a mix of images and phrases from magazines, newspapers, gift-wrap, or whatever, find images that represent **you** when you are not in control or when you feel "powerless." On the next page, paste things that represent you when you feel **proud** and **powerful.** Write about what makes the difference between the two.

ORVIDAS

Action | Reaction

Every now and then, things happen that bring up bad memories. These things are sometimes called "triggers." We can't always control things around us or the way others behave, but we do have a choice about whether we **REACT** out of fear or **RESPOND** from a healthy place.

Think about some things that trigger you and how you typically react to them — in your mind, heart and body.

Do you get upset, do you think badly about yourself, do you deal with it and move on? Do you like how you respond? What tends to happen when you respond that way? Is there anything you would like to change about your reaction? Why or why not?

Come up with a few ideas of how you could choose to react differently and decide what might work best in the future. Make a chart like this one to help you figure things out:

Event	Emotional or Physical Reaction	Action	A Second Chance
(trigger)	(feeling)	(choice)	(new response)
When I hear you raise your voice,	my stomach ties into knots because it reminds me of ___.	Then I slam the door and I ___.	But really, I want to ___ instead...
When you ___	I feel ___	I ___ and ___	I want to ___ instead

23

Dreams can bring us closer to our thoughts and feelings, help solve problems, make decisions easier, and encourage us to overcome our fears. Sometimes it's hard to recall our dreams, but by keeping this book and a pen by your bedside, you can get in the habit of writing them down while they're still fresh.

As soon as you wake up, keep your eyes closed and stay still. Reflect on the thoughts and feelings you may still have from your dream. Now open your eyes and write down any impressions, words, images, themes, places, textures, colors, etc. that pop into your head.

Do this over and over during the next few weeks, and watch for repeated images or themes. Are there any scenes or characters that keep popping up? Are you active in the dream or watching from the sidelines? If your dream became a movie, what would the title be? Ask yourself questions to help you unravel any hidden meanings and symbols.

Artwork by Mike McMillen

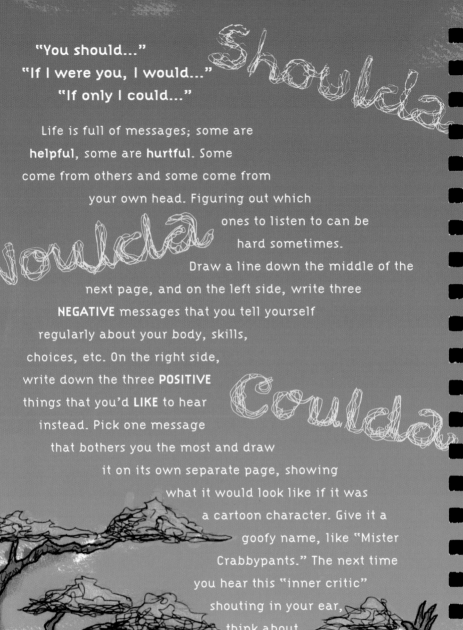

"You should..."
"If I were you, I would..."
"If only I could..."

Shoulda

Life is full of messages; some are
helpful, some are **hurtful**. Some
come from others and some come from
your own head. Figuring out which
ones to listen to can be
hard sometimes.
Draw a line down the middle of the
next page, and on the left side, write three
NEGATIVE messages that you tell yourself
regularly about your body, skills,
choices, etc. On the right side,
write down the three **POSITIVE**
things that you'd **LIKE** to hear
instead. Pick one message
that bothers you the most and draw
it on its own separate page, showing
what it would look like if it was
a cartoon character. Give it a
goofy name, like "Mister
Crabbypants." The next time
you hear this "inner critic"
shouting in your ear,
think about
how silly he looks
and tell him "Hasta La
Vista, Baby!"

Woulda

Coulda

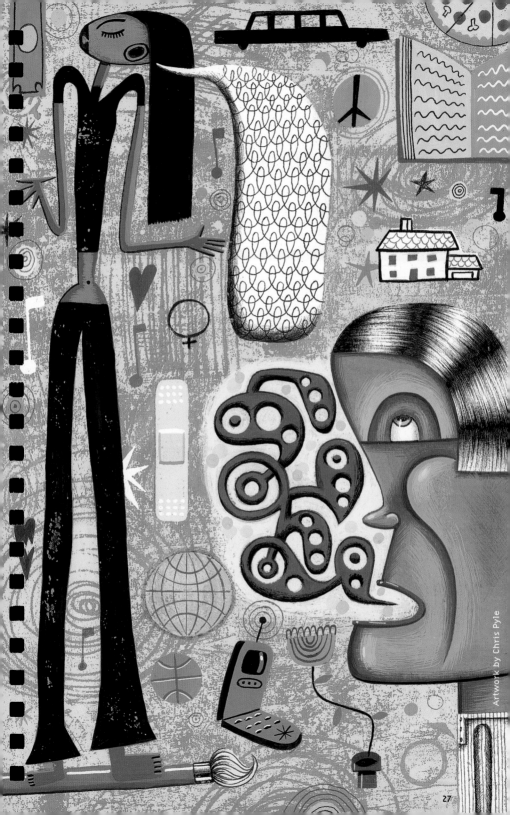

Artwork by Chris Pyle

THE LAST WORD

Sometimes, you don't get to say everything you wanted to say. Some things are left unsaid. Here are some prompts to help you write a letter where you can spill your guts. When you are finished writing it, tear it out, tear it up, and throw it away so that **YOU** can have the last word. Use the other blank pages to write to **ANYONE**, any place or any situation you want to say goodbye to (like a bad habit, an old school, or...?).

Dear ____,

When you left, I felt ____. What I really wanted to say, but didn't, was ____ because ____.

I remember the time when ____.

You know, that made me feel ____.

If we could speak face to face right now, I would say ____. I wish that ____. If I could, I would ____.

I am sorry about ____. I resent ___ but I appreciate ____. One thing I've learned since then is ____.

I feel like I've lost ____, but gained ____. Thank you for ____.

Bridges

TURN THE BOOK ONTO ITS SIDE, so it's horizontal. On the left side of the blank page, draw the situation you are in, showing a concern or problem you are dealing with right now. On the right side of the paper, draw where you **WANT TO BE,** with the problem solved.

Now, draw a bridge that moves you from the problem to the solution. Write down what you would be thinking, feeling, and doing differently once you arrive on the other side.

OUR HEROES

Artwork by Zaara KittenChops

This 4th reprint of Chill & Spill has been underwritten by generous contributions from:

Personal Safety Nets®

THE BRADLEY FAMILY FOUNDATION

Written by Steffanie Lorig and Jeanean Jacobs, MA, ATR-BC, LPAT, CPC

Design and hand-rendered titles by Andrew Wicklund • **Illustrations** by 20 amazing artists • **Concept & Art Direction** by Steffanie Lorig

PRINTED ON ENVIRONMENTALLY CONSCIOUS PAPERS

JEANEAN WOULD LIKE TO THANK her mentors Jan Edwards, ATR-BC, LMFT, Marcia Rosal, PhD, ATR-BC, Dr. Sandra Graves, PhD, ATR-BC, Abby Calisch, Psy.D. ATR, her friend Jane Tillman, LHMC, her mother Jacqueline Douglas, as well as Art with Heart for this opportunity.

STEFFANIE WOULD LIKE TO THANK: Judy Pigott, Carl Bradley, Kathy L. Goodwin, Scott Serna, Jeanean Jacobs, Linda Baker, Gary Helling, Annie McCall, Andrew Wicklund, Rosalie Frankel, Ron Rabin, Joe Isaak, Mary Murray, Anne Basham, Zandi Salstrom, and last but not least, Rick and Asher Lorig.

BIOGRAPHIES

Check out the stories of the excellent folks who
donated their time and talent to this book:

Darren Booth ✏️ Darren is a Canadian illustrator who has been drawing and painting pictures since he was little. He graduated from Sheridan College and has been working professionally since 2001 for clients such as ESPN, New York Magazine, Ladies Home Journal, Continental Airlines and others. He enjoys drawing animals, words and people. His patchwork style is executed traditionally by hand (meaning "not on the computer"). www.darrenbooth.com

Joe Ciardiello ✏️ Joe loves to draw and has been making pictures since the age of 4. He grew up on Staten Island, just a short ferry ride from Manhattan, where he attended both high school and college. Since then, his illustrations have appeared in many magazines (like Rolling Stone), books and on CD covers. He particularly enjoys drawing musicians, since he is a drummer himself. Joe lives in a 180-year-old house in western New Jersey. www.joeciardiello.com

Elizabeth Haidle ✏️ After coming of age in the suburbs of Portland, Oregon, Elizabeth Haidle launched her artistic adventure in various cities: New Mexico, Seattle, Philadelphia, L.A., Savannah... eventually earning an MA in Illustration. She has dabbled in opportunities involving art therapy, animation, gallery exhibition, and rock stars. Current projects include a quarterly non-fiction booklet entitled, "ComiCosmos" and a children's book series about extremely slow animals. Right now, she, her child and hedgehog live in Taos. www.ehaidle.com and www.MinutiaeLabs.com

Jeanean Jacobs ✏️ Jeanean is a national board certified, licensed Art Therapist and Certified Professional Life Coach. She is the Director of In-Home Programs at a nonprofit in Louisville, Kentucky helping to provide stability, hope and healing to foster children and their families. She's passionate about supporting opportunities for people to restore self-assurance, expand possibility and thrive. Her superheroes include Xena, Rumi and Carl Jung.

Mary Jones ✏️ Mary has illustrated three books for kids and has done illustrations for companies like The Chicago Tribune, Utne Reader and The Great Books Foundation. She exhibits paintings, prints and artists' books in galleries in Chicago and Milwaukee and currently lives in the Des Moines, Iowa area, where she teaches at Grand View University. www.maryjonesart.com

David Lemley ✏️ David journals almost everyday when he first wakes up. This helps him to get over the fact that he lost the eighth grade talent show right about the time he chose drawing and writing over singing and bashing guitars into amps. His kids often ask him to grow up and act like a normal dad because he still sings off-key really loud in the car and pretends to hold a microphone while steering.

Steffanie Lorig ➾ Steffanie was shy and awkward as a child, and used art to express herself. She was always doodling in the margins during class and making funky sculptures out of trash. Her best grades were always in Art and English, and when she grew up, she went to college to learn to became a graphic designer. After doing that for over a decade, she discovered that what she really wanted to do was use her skills to help kids. In 1996, she started Art with Heart and now gets to combine her skills and passion to create books like this one. Her other books include "Oodles of Doodles" and "Magnificent Marvelous Me." She and her husband co-wrote a children's book called "Such a Silly Baby" that parents, kids, and even the New York Times liked! She is still shy, but pretends she's not. www.artwithheart.org and www.lorigland.com

Mike McMillen ➾ Mike enjoyed all the usual childhood stuff until the age of 14, when he had his eye shot out by a BB gun. Because of the accident, he had to work his tail off to graduate on time from high school since he missed a semester's worth of classes. Luckily, he graduated with his friends and eventually ended up at the Art Institute of Seattle where he finally got homework that was fun. After landing an internship as a computer artist for video games, he spent the next nine years happily doing character design, modeling and animation. When his dad died, he was named President of the Robert B. McMillen Foundation, and now has the best job in the world. In his spare time, he enjoys scuba diving and making jewelry. www.mcmillenfoundation.org

Dushan Milic ➾ Dushan is an award-winning illustrator from Canada that wallows in word play and maddening colors. Cubists, cartoons, signage, punk, people, and puns inspire him. His highly stylized work has appeared in many newspapers and magazines. He used to be an art director, but now his time is spent solely on freelance illustration and design. He enjoys his work like nobody's business. www.dushanmilic.com

Ken Orvidas ➾ Ken lives and works in the Seattle area. He is married, has 2 kids, 3 cats and 2 dogs. For his award-winning, conceptual illustrations, he uses pencil, acrylic paint or pastel, sometimes adding "found objects" and textures into his work. Then he scans it all in and manipulates it until it's 'just right.' His global clients range from leading magazines to newspapers, corporations to book publishers, design firms to advertising agencies and he hopes to work on more books for kids. While not illustrating, he creates metal sculptures, cooks fancy-pants food and labors in several gardens around his house. www.orvidas.com

Chris Pyle ➾ Chris' mom was a Renaissance woman who loved all forms of the arts. She shared her interest with Chris and was the first to recognize his talents. For his 6th grade history class, he drew Egyptian hieroglyphics and people. When his mom saw it, she immediately enrolled him in a painting class with adults! Her encouragement helped ignite his spark of talent. Chris now lives in Indianapolis and spends his day as an illustrator and jazz musician. His influences range from Picasso to Tex Avery to his wife and son. He has doodled for clients such as Coca Cola, Time, Rolling Stone, Entertainment Weekly, New York Magazine and TV Guide. And the illustration he did for this book won a cool art prize! www.chrispyleillustration.com

Lynn Rowe Reed ➾ Lynn lives in Indiana, has two art degrees, two kids, no pets and eleven books, including the critically-acclaimed "Punctuation Takes A Vacation." Lynn's quirky, contemporary style is fresh and engaging to folks of all ages. In 2004, the New York Times said that her "childlike acrylic paintings perfectly capture the mood of whimsical fantasy." Lynn works from a studio in a very old brick building that was once a mill. She recently put a basketball hoop on her door to help stir creative energy in moments of blandness and indecision. www.lynnrowereed.com

Lilla Rogers ➾ Lilla is an internationally known illustrator and painter, and owner of a successful illustration agency. Her work has been seen in hundreds of magazines and has been exhibited in shows worldwide. Her clients have included Levi Jeans, Rolling Stone, Chronicle Books, CBS Records, Electra Records, L'Oreal, Esteé Lauder, Showtime, Disney and more. Lilla currently lives in New England with her husband and 2 children. www.lillarogers.com

Mark T. Smith ✏️ Mark is one of New York City's most influential artists. He has created over 600 paintings and thousands of drawings. His subject matter is as diverse as his pallet, ranging from heroes to hot rods, Christianity to cowboys. He has done work for Taco Bell, Walt Disney Company, MTV, ShowTime Networks, Nickelodeon, Pepsi-Co and dozens other companies. His national goal is to take art out into public spaces, where everyone can have a chance to enjoy it. www.marktsmith.com

Katherine Streeter ✏️ Katherine is an illustrator living in New York City, where she finds lots of old and fun pieces to use in her collage art. Her collection of antique dolls and magazines inspires her work in the studio. When she is out of the studio, her favorite pastime is playing with Olive her dog. She has done lots of work for various magazines, like The New York Times, Bloomberg and Shape, as well as for book publishers and music clients. She has several awards behind her name and her art has been exhibited globally. www.katherinestreeter.com

Mark Todd ✏️ Mark graduated with honors from Art Center College of Design in Pasadena and then moved to New York where he worked for clients like MTV, Coca-Cola, Sony Music and The New Yorker. Mark has written and illustrated three books for children, including MONSTER TRUCKS! (Houghton Mifflin). Mark lives in sunny southern California with his wife and fellow artist, Esther Pearl Watson and their daughter Lili, an avid artist herself. Mark and Esther co-teach illustration classes and they have a cool book for teens that teaches how to create 'zines and mini-comics (Houghton Mifflin). www.marktoddillustration.com

Gina Triplett ✏️ Gina is an artist whose work ends up in galleries, magazines and other cool places, like Surfer Magazine, Rolling Stone, Target, Converse, Urban Outfitters and Chronicle Books. She shares her studio with her husband, Matt, and her scrappy Boston Terrier named Wesley in Philadelphia, the land of cheesesteaks, the Liberty Bell, and good ole Ben Franklin himself. When not painting, she gardens and rides her bike to get coffee. www.ginaandmatt.com

Andrew Wicklund ✏️ Andrew's first 21 years of life as a Midwest kid were spent playing sports and drawing. He figured that was what all other kids did too, and was shocked to find that wasn't necessarily true. That realization fueled his desire to travel, learn about different cultures, and share his love of creativity with others. Now, after 35 years on this planet, he uses one of his childhood passions to make a living as a graphic designer and illustrator and enjoys meeting others along this exciting journey.

Nate Williams ✏️ Nate had a learning disability when he was young so reading didn't make much sense to him. He responded better to imagery he saw on skateboards, food packaging, stickers, Dr. Seuss, and Shel Silverstein. He was hyper and didn't have the patience to sit down and read, so it was a quick way to figure it all out. Originally from western U.S., Nate currently lives in South/Central America and works as an illustrator and artist. www.n8w.com

Zaara KittenChops (Marta Windeisen) ✏️ Zaara was born and raised in Hungary (you know: Zsazsa Gabor, Goulash, Rubik's Cube...). After earning her Bachelor of Arts in Design at Western Washington University, she worked at the Starbuck's national headquarters in-house design studio for five years. Now she runs her own business, specializing in design and illustration filled with Heart Opening Energy. Her sources of inspiration include her two cats, Bollywood movies, Japanese magazines and packaging, reading and collecting books. www.kittenchops.com

Laura Zeck ✏️ Laura first discovered printmaking at Field Day in the third grade and was thoroughly unimpressed. Later in college, she lost a bet to a friend — the loser was forced to take a class of the winner's choice. Her friend chose a printmaking class for her and it actually wasn't so bad. Soon it became her medium of choice. Sounds simple, eh? But between then and now, she has been an art teacher, waitress, writer, art director, waitress, photographer, and headhunter...until she finally got back into printmaking. Today she works in her studio with a tiny dog to keep her company. www.laurazeck.com/shortstories

So, what did you think about Chill & Spill?

Fill in this side, and then use the other side to draw how this book made you feel. Fold, seal, stick on a stamp and mail it to us. We can't wait to hear from you!

My name is _____. I am _____ years old.

I struggle with _____

_____

_____

Before I started using Chill & Spill, I felt (circle one):

| Pissed-Off | Crappy | Worried | Sad | Okay | Content | Happy |

After I finished Chill & Spill, I felt (circle one):

| Pissed-Off | Crappy | Worried | Sad | Okay | Content | Happy |

Chill & Spill helped me (check all that apply):

❑ express or figure out my feelings ❑ feel better about myself or my situation
❑ make better choices ❑ see things about myself I wasn't aware of before
❑ share things about myself with others ❑ other_____

Chill & Spill also helped me _____

_____

_____

_____

_____

_____

I'd also like to say: _____

_____

_____

C&S 4th printing 2013

NAME/RETURN ADDRESS:

_____

_____

_____

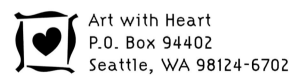

Art with Heart
P.O. Box 94402
Seattle, WA 98124-6702